Step-by-step **kawaii** creatu

The
Super
Cute
Drawing Book

Tanya
Emelyanova

ARCTURUS

ARCTURUS

This edition published in 2019 by Arcturus Publishing Limited
26/27 Bickels Yard, 151–153 Bermondsey Street,
London SE1 3HA

Copyright © Arcturus Holdings Limited

All rights reserved. No part of this publication may be reproduced,
stored in a retrieval system, or transmitted, in any form or by
any means, electronic, mechanical, photocopying, recording or
otherwise, without prior written permission in accordance with the
provisions of the Copyright Act 1956 (as amended). Any person or
persons who do any unauthorized act in relation to this publication
may be liable to criminal prosecution and civil claims for damages.

Illustrated by Tanya Emelyanova
Written by William Potter
Edited by Joe Harris
Designed by squareandcircus.co.uk

ISBN: 978-1-78950-623-5
CH007141NT
Supplier 29, Date 0919, Print run 8920

Printed in China

CONTENTS

What is Kawaii?

Kawaii is cuteness!

Kawaii started out in Japan in the 1970s. Originally, it just meant "cute," but today kawaii has become a cool style of art and fashion that's popular all over the world.

Kawaii is all about fun, cheekiness, friendship, and laughter ... but most of all, cuteness. Just follow the fun projects in this book, and soon you will be able to make anything adorable!

Kawaii characters are simple to draw, with large round heads, dots for eyes, tiny noses and smiles, all in pastel shades. You can add a kawaii face to just about anything.

Back to Basics

You can draw kawaii with any pencils or pens, but we suggest drawing a light pencil outline, then going over it with crayon to match the shades you want.

Here are some different faces you can use on your super-cute characters to show different moods and personalities.

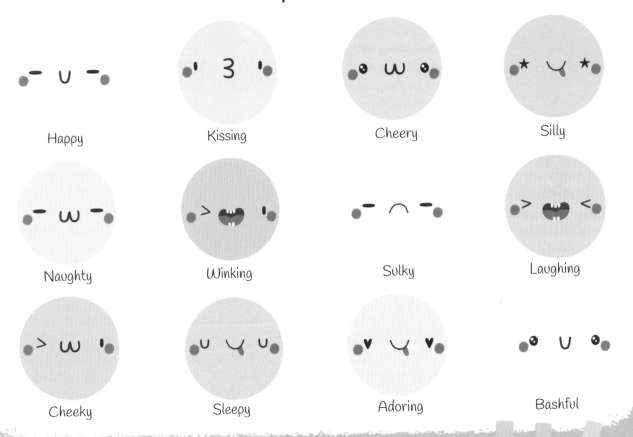

Happy	Kissing	Cheery	Silly
Naughty	Winking	Sulky	Laughing
Cheeky	Sleepy	Adoring	Bashful

For extra cuteness , draw large dark eyes with white dots for reflections, plus rosy cheeks.

You can add other details to the faces, then decorate with hearts and stars, but keep it simple!

Follow the steps in this book, copy the drawings into the scenes, then invent your own super-cute characters to fill sketchbooks with oodles of doodles!

Adorable ANIMALS

Cuddly Kitten

Follow the steps to draw a cute, curled-up kitten.

1

2

3

4

Just Fur Fun!
Try giving each of your cats a different fur pattern.

It's playtime! Draw some kitties with their toys.

Honey Bunny

Follow the steps to draw this friendly rabbit. Doesn't she look huggable?

Rabbits Love Company!
Draw some friends
for Honey Bunny!

Add some cheeky rabbits to this vegetable patch!

turnip

carrot

cabbage

radish

Perfect Panda

Have a go at drawing this hungry panda feeding on a bamboo shoot.

1

2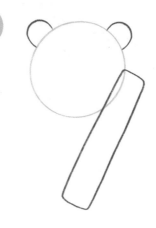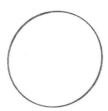

3

4

5

6

Add plenty of pandas in the jungle.
There's so much bamboo to chew!

13

Playful Puppy

Follow the simple steps to draw your own pet puppy.

Best in Show!
Give each dog its own collar, bow, or scarf.

Take your puppy to the park, and draw lots of friends for him to play with.

Dinky Duck

Here's how to draw an adorable duck.

1

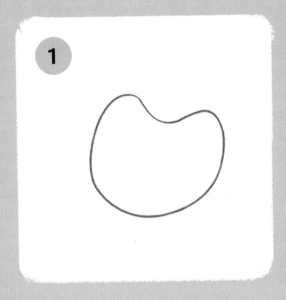

2

3

4

Ducks love to splash about.
Draw some paddling in this pond.

17

Loveable Llama

Follow the steps to draw a wonderful, woolly llama.

1

2

3

4

Flower Friends
Add lots of bees and butterflies buzzing about the blooms.

Now, fill this field with a group of
happy-go-lucky llamas.

Snoozy Red Panda

It's nap time for this adorable red panda cub. Follow the steps to draw her.

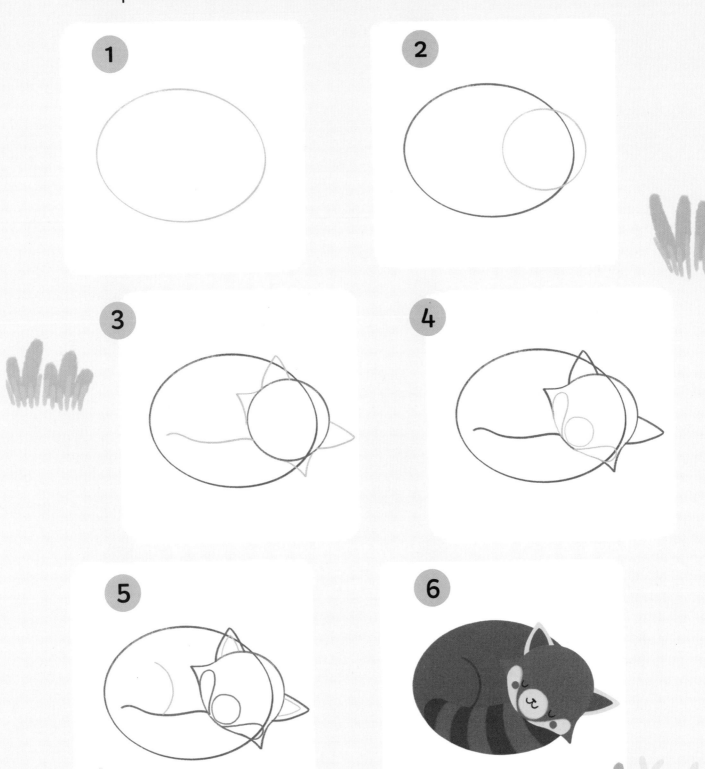

Add some sleepy red panda cubs snoozing beside their mother.

Perky Penguin

Draw a prize-winning penguin following these four simple steps.

Winter Wear
Keep your penguins extra-warm with some winter woollies.

Add several penguins skating in this snowy scene.

Happy Hamster

Here's how to draw a handsome hamster, one step at a time.

Now draw lots of furry hamsters at play together.

Splashing Seal

Follow the steps to draw a sweet seal pup.

Now add some seals swimming about in the sea.

Make a Move

Try drawing your cute
creatures in different poses.
Here are some animals in action.

Tasty TREATS

Yummy Cupcakes

Follow the steps to draw a cute cupcake.

Top Toppings
What will you choose to
add to your cupcake?

Fill this cake-shop window with lots of delicious cupcakes.

BAKERY SHOP

Ice Cream

On a hot, sunny day, there's nothing nicer than enjoying an ice cream!

1

2

Even Sweeter

Here are some tasty toppings to add.

3

Add some ice creams to the display. What will you choose—vanilla, strawberry, or chocolate?

Hot Cocoa

Need warming up? Draw a cute cup of cocoa!

A Little Extra
Do you need something sweeter? Why not add cream or marshmallows!

Your order's ready! Draw several full cups of
cocoa on the tray.

Iced Donuts

Follow the steps to cook up some delicious donuts.

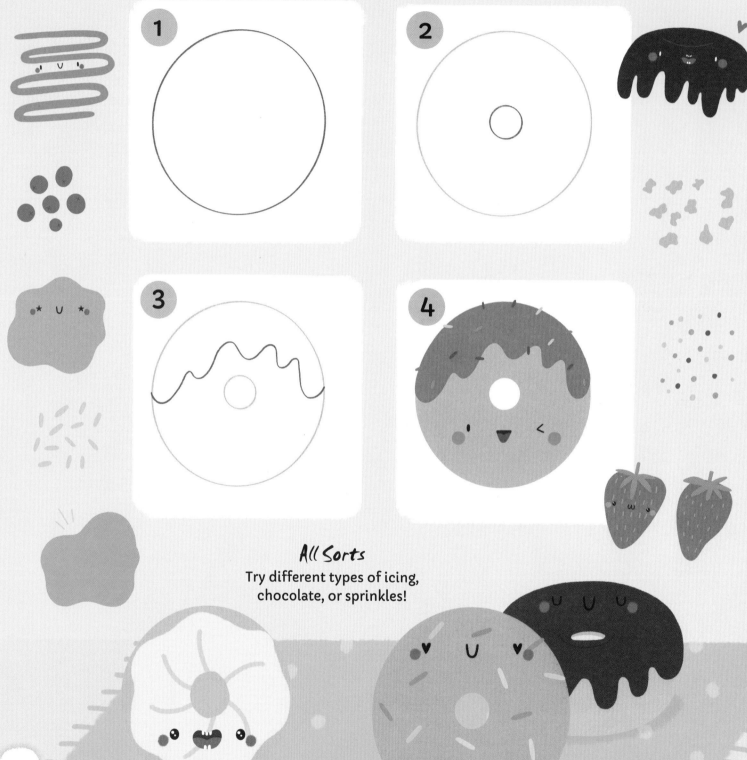

All Sorts
Try different types of icing,
chocolate, or sprinkles!

Juicy Pineapple

Here's how to draw a perfect pineapple for a fruit family.

Fruit Faces
Here are some faces you can add to the fruit.

Add cute faces to all the fabulous fruit on this page.

Steamed Dumplings

Follow the steps to dish up a delicious dumpling!

1

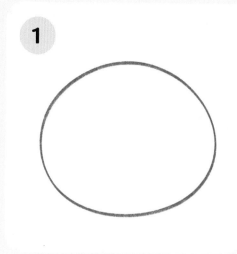

2

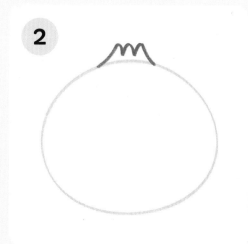

3

Now, draw some dumplings on the plate, ready to share!

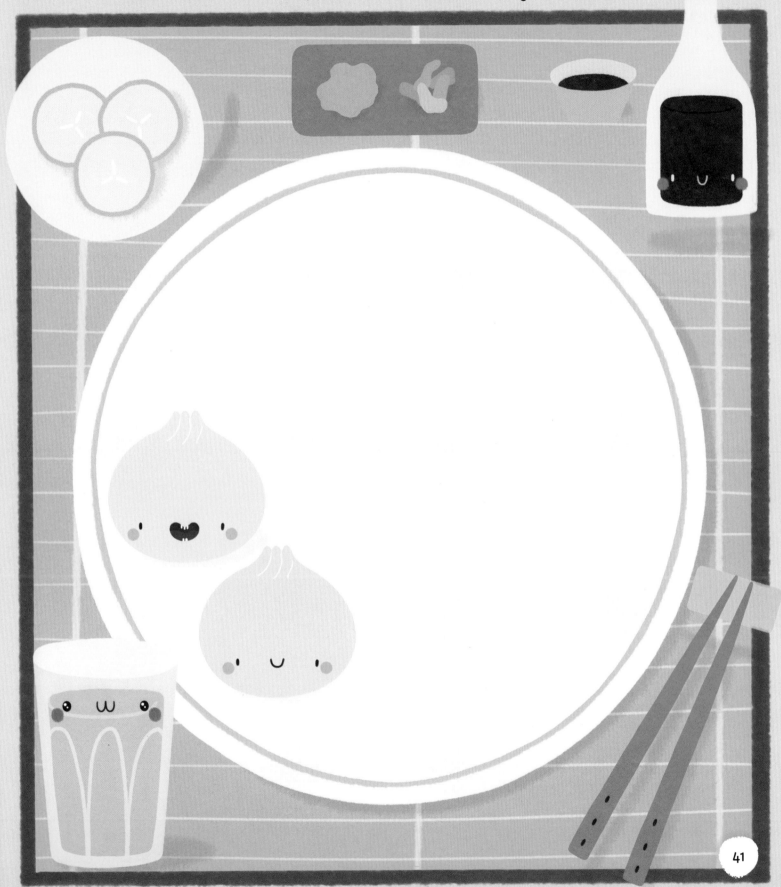

Peas in a Pod

Take your pick! Here's a pod full of peas for you to draw.

1

2

3

4

Veggie Pals
Here are some faces you can add to the vegetables.

Add some funny faces to the vegetable basket!

Sticky Sushi

Step right up for a simply super sushi draw!

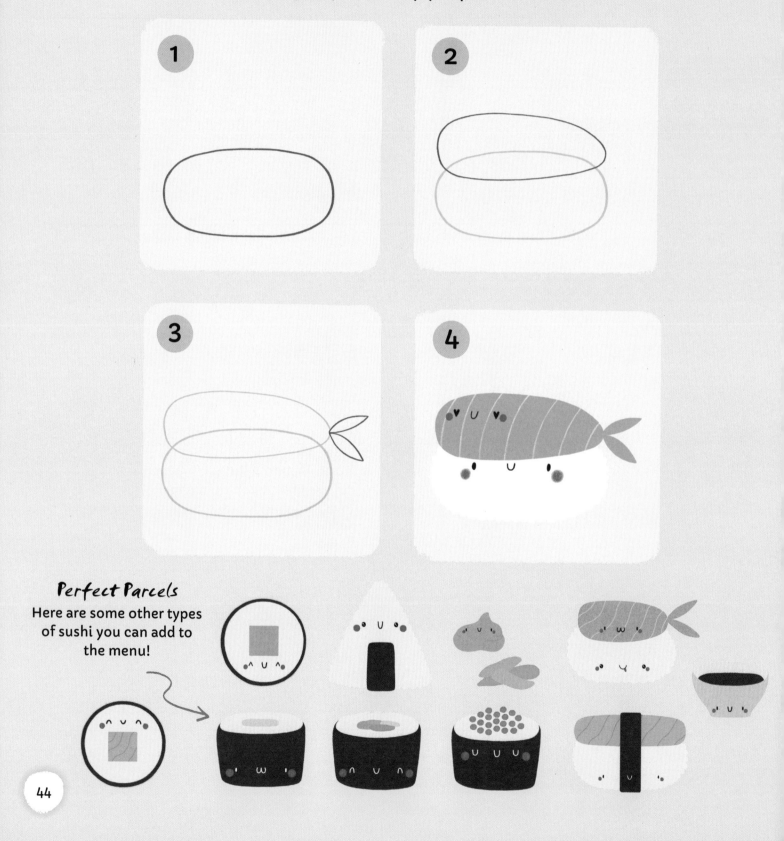

Perfect Parcels

Here are some other types of sushi you can add to the menu!

Neatly place your sushi on the board ready for picking.

Tasty Burger

Create your own perfect burger by following the simple steps.

Build up your burgers, adding lettuce, cheese, tomatoes, and sauces too!

Slurpy Noodles

Time for a yummy bowl of noodles! Follow the steps to draw this dish.

Chef's Choice
Add whatever you like to your noodle dishes. Here are some ideas.

Who's hungry? Give these jolly diners each a bowl of healthy noodles.

49

Yum Yum!

Add some cute faces to these tasty treats.

Just IMAGINE

Dancing Unicorn

Here's how to bring a magical unicorn to life, one step at a time.

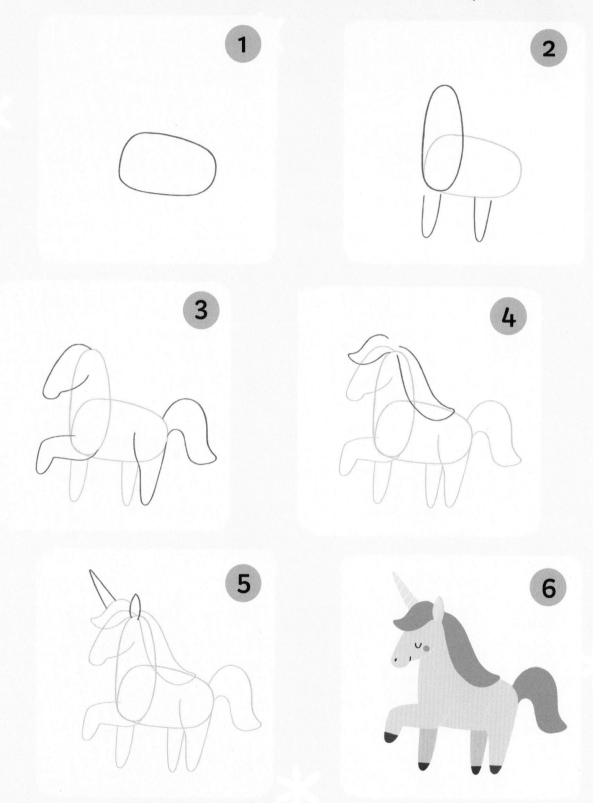

Draw some amazing unicorns trotting about in this fantasy land.

53

Flower Fairy

Magic up a fluttering flower fairy following these simple steps.

1

2

3

4

5

6

Fairyland Faces
Here are some faces you can add to your fairies.

Draw some flower fairies in their secret woodland home.

Baby Dragon

Here's how to bring a baby dragon to life.

Add several young dragons
guarding their cave of crystals.

Kindly Witch

Wave your pencil like a magic wand and draw a wonderful witch.

Hey, Presto! Make your witches more magical with these spooky extras.

Draw a witch for every broomstick
in the night sky.

Tiny Dinosaur

Roarrrr! Follow the steps to draw a tiny but noisy dinosaur.

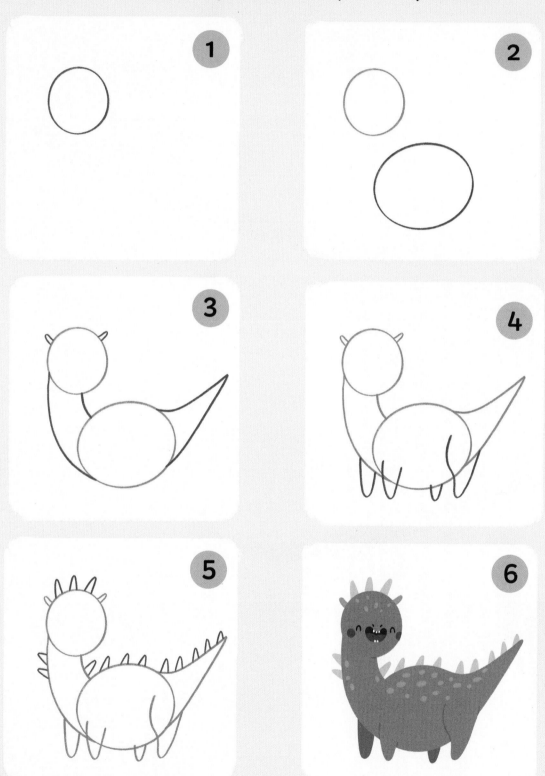

Draw loads of dinosaurs prowling this prehistoric land.

Dancing Princess

Want to draw a pretty princess? Give it a twirl!

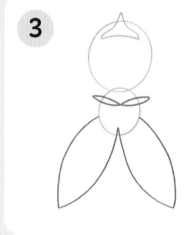

Draw some royal guests dancing at the palace ball.

Helpful Robot

Help is at hand with this clanking robot. Follow the steps to build him.

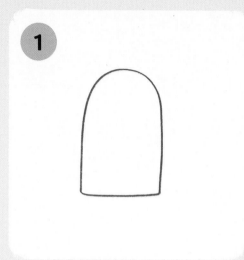

Draw some cute robots in the workshop. You can add any parts you want.

Little Ninja

Hi-ya! This teeny ninja has quite a kick!

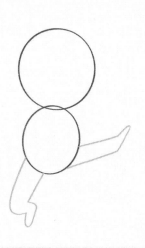

The little ninjas are in a big battle.
Draw them leaping over the rooftops.

Mini Monster

Go wild drawing a mad monster, following the simple steps.

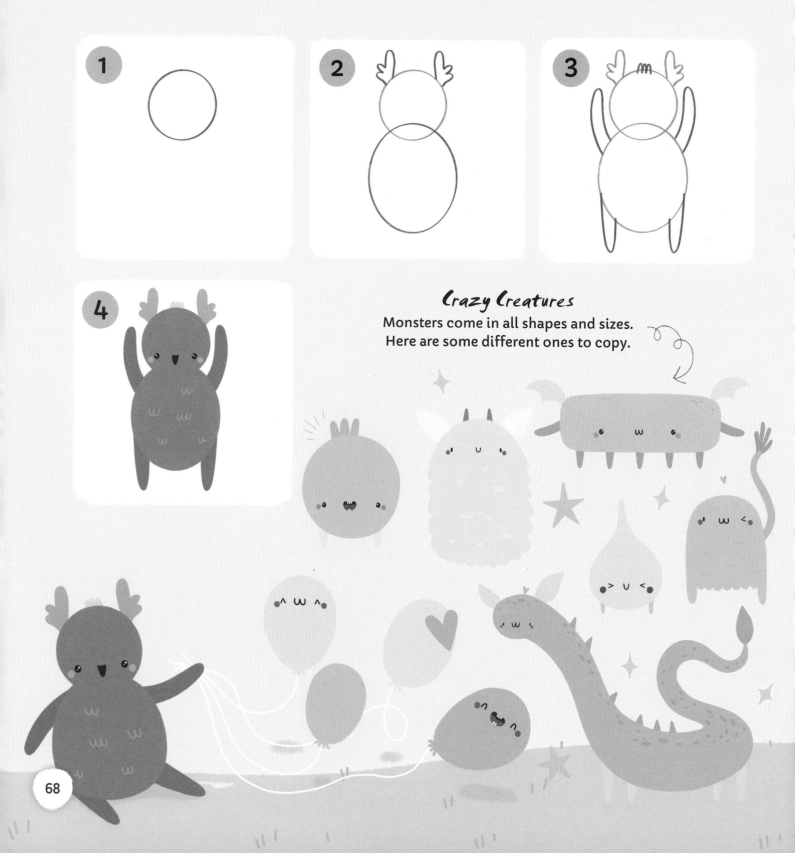

1

2

3

4

Crazy Creatures

Monsters come in all shapes and sizes. Here are some different ones to copy.

Watch out! There are monsters about!
Draw them stomping in this scene.

Goofy Ghost

Don't be frightened by this silly ghost! Try drawing him instead.

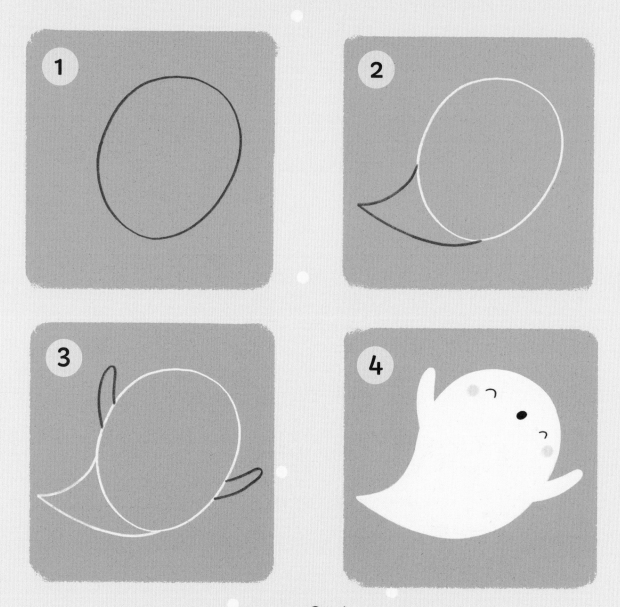

Say Boo!
Give your ghosts one of these funny faces.

Where's the scare? Draw lots of cute ghosts hiding in this haunted house.

71

Jam-packed!

Have fun filling this page with kawaii
doodles of your own. We've made
a start for you.

Chibi
CITY

Chirpy Chef

What's cooking? Follow the steps to draw this cheeky chef.

There's lots of food to be prepared. Fill the kitchen with busy little chefs.

City Mayor

Meet the mayor. Draw the city leader one step at a time.

1

2

3

4

5

6

The mayor has to give an important speech. Draw her on the steps of the city hall.

Baseball Player

Here's how to draw an ace baseball player for the big game.

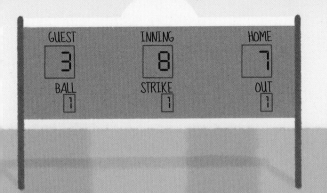

GUEST
3
BALL
1

INNING
8
STRIKE
1

HOME
7
OUT
1

Now, assemble your baseball team on the field.

Amazing Astronaut

Follow the steps to draw an out-of-this-world astronaut.

1

2

3

4

5

6

In Orbit
Add some stars, planets, and rocket ships to
your outer-space scene.

Time to go on a spacewalk.
Draw some astronauts working near the space station.

81

Pizza Delivery

Who ordered pizza? Try drawing this delivery boy.

1

2

3

4

5

6

This shop has lots of pizzas ready to send out.
Draw some pizza-delivery boys and girls with their bikes.

Busy Builder

Here's how to build your own clever construction worker.

1

2

3

4

5

6

This skyscraper won't build itself!
Add lots of builders at work on the site.

Racing Driver

Get your drawing skills in gear by drawing this daring racing driver.

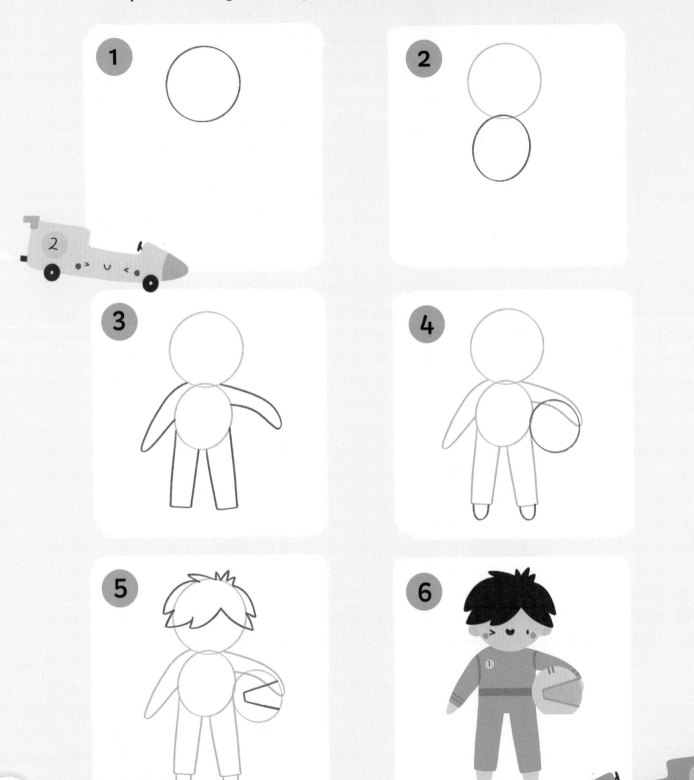

The race cars are on the track.
They just need you to add drivers!

Kind Nurse

Follow the steps to draw a fun and friendly nurse.

1

2

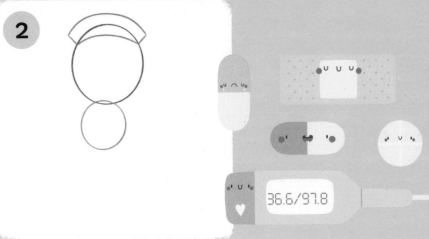

3

4

First-Aid Kit
Give your nurses the kit to help them help others.

5

6

Singing Star

Here's how to draw a superstar singer in six easy steps.

1

2

3

4

5
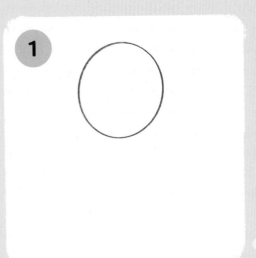

6

It's karaoke time! Draw some superstars on stage, singing the hits.

Friendly Farmer

Follow the steps to draw a funny farmer ready to tend the animals.

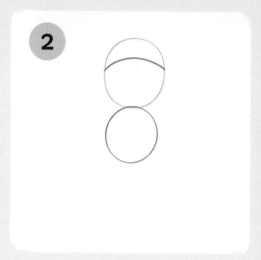

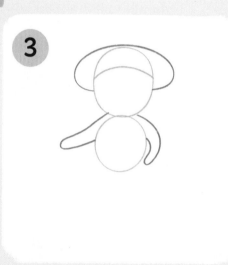

Now add some farmers working on the farm.

Jobs to Do

There are lots of jobs to do in the city.
Here are some uniforms and tools for you to copy.

Wonderful World

Your kawaii people need somewhere to live! Here are some doodles you can add to your city scenes.

Super City

Now doodle your own super-cute city.
We've made a start for you.